A FORM OF OPTIMISM

Other volumes in the series:

The Morse Poetry Prize • *Edited by Guy Rotella*

A FORM OF OPTIMISM

Roy Jacobstein

THE 2006 MORSE POETRY PRIZE

Selected and introduced by Lucia Perillo

Northeastern University Press
BOSTON

PUBLISHED BY UNIVERSITY PRESS OF NEW ENGLAND
HANOVER AND LONDON

Northeastern University Press
Published by University Press of New England,
One Court Street, Lebanon, NH 03766
www.upne.com
© 2006 by Roy Jacobstein
Printed in the United States of America
5 4 3 2 1

The author gratefully acknowledges permission to reprint the following:
Agha Shahid Ali, lines from "The Dacca Gauzes" from *The Half Inch Himalayas* © 1987
by Agha Shahid Ali and reprinted by permission of Wesleyan University Press.

Library of Congress Cataloging-in-Publication Data
Jacobstein, Roy.
A form of optimism / Roy Jacobstein ; selected and introduced by Lucia Perillo.
    p.   cm. — (The 2006 Morse Poetry Prize)
ISBN-13: 978–1–55553–664–0 (cloth : alk. paper)
ISBN-10: 1–55553–664–6 (cloth : alk. paper)
ISBN-13: 978–1–55553–665–7 (pbk. : alk. paper)
ISBN-10: 1–55553–665–4 (pbk. : alk. paper)
  I. Perillo, Lucia Maria, 1958– II. Title. III. Series: Morse Poetry Prize ; 2006.
PS3610.A3568F67 2006
811'.6—dc22   2006013898

 University Press of New England is a member of the Green Press
Initiative. The paper used in this book meets their minimum require-
ment for recycled paper.

For Linda, di nuòvo

Yet men will murder among holy days;
Thou must hold water in a witch's sieve . . .
—John Keats, "The Eve of St. Agnes"

Contents

Acknowledgments

Grateful acknowledgment is made to the editors of the following publications where these poems, some of them since revised, first appeared:

Arts & Letters: "The Dog Races in Florida," "Emigrées," "Knowing Insomnia," "Sound and Light"
Crab Orchard Review: "The Word"
The Gettysburg Review: "Embarkation"
Indiana Review: "Decimation," "The Mystery and Melancholy of the Street," "Peach Time, Nepal," "Sighting"
Many Mountains Moving: "Mosaic: Istanbul"
The Marlboro Review: "A Form of Optimism," "Western History"
Mid-American Review: "Jewel Case," "Moe," "Mother Teresa and I Are Upgraded to First Class"
Nimrod: "Spastic"
Prairie Schooner: "Correspondence," "Grace," "Heel," "HIV Needs Assessment," "Immortality," "Scariest Movie"
Quarterly West: "Depth of Field"
Rivendell: "We Called Him *Dost*"
The Threepenny Review: "Ardor," "Don't You Love Spanish"
TriQuarterly: "One Another"
Witness: "Anecdotal Evidence"

"Ardor" was featured on *Poetry Daily.*
"Don't You Love Spanish," "Grace" and "We Called Him *Dost*" appear in the chapbook *Tourniquet* (Hollyridge Press, 2005).
The six poems that appeared in *Prairie Schooner* were selected by its editors for the 2006 Glenna Luschei *Prairie Schooner* Award.
"Anecdotal Evidence" is anthologized in *Under the Rock Umbrella: Modern American Poets* (Mercer University Press, 2006).
"The Mystery and Melancholy of the Street" is included in the textbook *LITERATURE: Reading Fiction, Poetry & Drama* (McGraw-Hill, 2006).

Introduction

"Poetry makes nothing happen"—so goes the old chestnut put into play by W. H. Auden. What he meant was that poetry that comes with a social agenda can easily slip into the harness of propaganda.

What does poetry do, then? What function can it serve? Especially now that life moves at a pace too accelerated to afford the kind of prolonged dream-time—in one of the outer islets of the cerebral archipelago—which is the kind of unfamiliar hammock-habitat that poetry demands.

One observation to be made concerns the word *witness* and how it got its due as an annoying verb in the latter part of the last millennium, a word used to describe the sometime work of poetry. Poetry, or so the story went, could serve to witness injustice in odd corners of the world. This gave rise to a kind of literary combat-tourism, with poets viewing war zones from the air-conditioned comfort of their rental cars. And some of these poems could shake a reader's bones, and did shake them. But, at the end of the day (or the century), poetry didn't do a lick of good when it came to shaping either foreign policy or the conventional wisdom. We prefer, it seems, reality television to reality.

As a poet and a doctor engaged in the field of public health, Roy Jacobstein observes the world—OK, witnesses—from a singularly important vantage. He has the rare authority to say of the AIDS crisis in Africa: "We've found the needs / many. But let us not talk of that, / as the people do not." And when the rental car rolls on (actually, Jacobstein rides in a "project vehicle"), he dwells not on the obvious and complicated politics of the virus but instead on the details that skitter away from the temptations of propaganda: "the lone ads for toothpaste / &

for study opportunity abroad, / & the many for caskets ('lightweight, / can be carried by one')."

What the doctors in the *project vehicle* finally say is nothing, as they ride past so much grief. Saying nothing is one response to the makes-nothing-happen problem raised by Auden. But, obviously, poetry *is* speech, or at least words on a page, and therefore a form of anti-silence. Which is a paradox, because poetry embraces silence too, what with all its peculiar white space.

Jacobstein dances down the center of these ambivalences, as a traveler as well as an invader, a suave member of the privileged class as well as a once-to-be-annihilated Jew, an American only a generation removed from the Old World, a do-gooder as well as a fucker-upper. As a result, *A Form of Optimism* leaves us informed as well as queasy, optimistic about the fate of the globe as well as trashed at heart. Jacobstein makes a song even about the weapons of our demise:

> Gatling and Colt,
> Mauser and Lüger,
> Kalashnikov, Uzi—

so that we remember that it was actual men who made and named them.

Poetry was created by the ancients in order to aid memory, so that memory could record *what had really happened* and carry it forth. But in our sophisticated modernism we know that deciding what really is happening ain't so easy. The poem can only put itself in the service of the moment, as Jacobstein realizes at the end of his travels through Turkey, a country near the center of our most urgent contentions:

> The rhythm of sands, of hawks and wells,
> reverberates like blood in a three-chambered heart,
> enters my arteries, murmurs
>
> *Even the now cannot be known.*

Nothing happens, nothing changes, but at least one moment is slipped into the recording ledger. Jacobstein knows that's all a poem can do, really—submit to the unknown now.

LUCIA PERILLO

ONE

A FORM OF OPTIMISM

I doze in tranches and planes,
    angled acutely
        like some Cubist harlequin.

Easy once, that nightly pirouette
    into REM sleep,
        but what with the road rage,

dirty bombs, malevolent spores,
    it's clear that's Oblivion
        whose sulfurous wheezes

are singeing our neck-hairs,
    hence my new habit
        of sleeping with the lights on—

which doesn't mean sleep's
    a bad thing, in fact
        its lack makes everyone's bones

cry out, and right now my vertebrae
    are emitting a cascade
        of wails to do a banshee proud.

O numinous world!, where a thing
    so routine, so banal
        as tonight's pastel sky

still takes one's breath, even as out there
    they're searching for the next
        seven-year-old stolen from her bed

while asleep, and cactuses in the desert
    (where the body waits)
        already are entering bloom.

EMIGRÉES

—*"Imagine the small empty purse
your mother carried across an ocean."*

Only now, in the airport waiting area,
riffling through a discarded *Redbook*
as our century passes its worn baton
to the next, do I vision her exodus

from Pilvestok, detritus of the First
World War. She'd have been three,
maybe four, already the trachoma
clouding her corneas, veiling her

from her own sight, threatening
to snuff the Statue's welcome lamp.
Did she grasp her Papa's hand the way
he grasped at prayer? And in her other

hand—what? A doll with blue clear eyes?
German fairy tales? Or perhaps a lemon,
its rough skin staining her palm for life,
so each time she touched hand to face

the next eight decades she'd inhale
that bitter scent, hear her sisters retching
again into the shadows of steerage,
and claw deeper into the hard ground.

DEPTH OF FIELD

Those bottle caps had a way of winking
        from the black tamped soil. That *Nehi*—
            how it shone, orange and white, brighter

than flame. Before my parents could claim
        their plot of grass by the city golf course,
            I was off, face bent low, an avid anteater

scanning the bounteous earth, left to right,
        then—*Eureka!*—pry it out with my stick,
            scud back to the blanket where he dozes,

off patrol: *Dad*, Army behind him, years
        of drift ahead. Flat gray sky, green greens,
            men in cleats thwacking hard white balls

(strays, exiles: numbered, pitted, rough).
        Got one, Mom! My fist opens to reveal *Faygo*
            Red Pop, carbonated taste of the Midwest;

her blouse closes over my nursing brother.
        Sturtevant Street sleeps too, there beneath
            its bittersweet blanket of burning leaves.

Our upstairs neighbor, Professor Roth,
        is still teaching Modern Chinese History
            at Wayne State—just a matter of time

until the loyalty oaths remake him
        a camera salesman, demonstrating
            the way the aperture is narrowed.

HEEL

Rhonda, my gentle and sturdy mix
of border collie and malamute,
who bears the endless probes
of two-year-olds with that good nature
bred into pack breeds, and limits her urgency
to the never ending, always futile quest
for squirrel and vole, who would smother
any burglar so grossly ill-informed
as to hope a cache of riches awaited him
with her wet nose and dangling tongue,
whose pacific acceptance of restraint
and rebuke is Buddhist and boundless,
has just torn for the throat of her fellow
mongrel, blind, gaunt, flatulent Maxx,
now-decrepit mutt my pal Alex retrieved
from the Shelter thirteen years ago and kept
serene mutual company with since—
as if Rhonda's malamute spine
and collie veins also felt the weight
of gravity pulling Maxx's frame
down, so for once she'd refused to obey
anybody's order to heel.

SCARIEST MOVIE

Growing up, the scariest movie
I ever saw was *Invisible Monster.*
This guy in a dark trenchcoat
and dark hat carried the monster
with him wherever he went,
in a hard-sided, snap-lock suitcase.
Every so often, to the dysphonic
strains of violins, he'd crack it open,
to give us a hint of its mighty force.
Hounds howled, lamp-posts toppled,
power lines hissed, we kids cowered
in the balcony. It was clear
there'd be no end to the havoc
should he open his suitcase wide.
Each night the unseen drove me
to the middle of my parents' bed,
twenty-three nights straight.
I can't recall the guy's face or voice,
but I swear he's still out there,
and my parents are dead.

SPASTIC

I could try to dodge the rain
of blows when the bullies struck
or flee should I see them first,

but what could he do, strapped
to his chair, except sit there aslant
that rubberized, yolk-yellow padding

as he was wheeled into Science
each morning, his head tracking
its slow, repetitive, delinquent path.

How good it felt to be a part
of the pack, anonymous, to pierce
the carapace of somebody else.

DON'T YOU LOVE SPANISH

Don't you love Spanish, how
it forewarns its questions.
Right away, you're alert—

ignorance around, they might
call on you and you know
you haven't read the book.

None of this being caught
unawares by some guttural
Teutonic tongue, suspended

until the end of the sentence,
when only then can you hope
to find you're off the hook.

EMBARKATION

Sudden thud at our feet:
man in gray suit,
face deepening purple
as if sluice gates
to a great dammed vat
of Merlot had opened wide.

Ticket in one hand,
briefcase in the other,
tie loose at his neck,
thirty seconds ago life
was making onward
connection. Now

memory depends
on five chest compressions
to each forced breath
and the rapid arrival
of the portable defibrillator—
and neither *TIME*

nor *National Geographic*'s
spread on Tierra del Fuego
seems of much interest
to the rest of us
waiting to board
our flight.

HIV NEEDS ASSESSMENT

Everywhere the faces, hair, limbs
    are coal, obsidian, flawless black
        sapphire, thus the rare *mzungu**

like me stands out the way those
    remaining white moths once did
        on industrialized London's trees.

A month fluttering *The Warm Heart*
    of Africa's long length on this *Needs*
        Assessment. We've found the needs

many. But let us not talk of that,
    as the people do not. Focus instead
        on the vivid oleander & limpid sky

that domes the arid volcanic hills,
    its lapis mirrored in the uniforms
        of the file of schoolgirls who stride

the side of the road. And when the talk,
    matter-of-fact, beyond resigned, bears
        left at the roundabout, glances upon

a cousin's funeral attended yesterday,
    the two added children your colleague
        from Lilongwe is now raising alone,

funeral venues for this weekend, just
    sit there as the *Project Vehicle* propels
        you onward to the next *Site*, past

the lone ads for toothpaste
    & for study opportunity abroad,
        & the many for caskets ("lightweight,

can be carried by one"), & say nothing.

*Swahili for *white person,* literally "to travel around"

TWO

DISCOVERY

They've reanimated the dinosaurs
    on the Discovery Channel, diplodocus,
        all eleven tons of double-beamed bulk

plus pecan brain scooting across the screen,
    vital and true. (Who among us can say not?)
        He's advanced from three-pound hatchling

cowering with his brood-mates beneath
    lush pre-Cambrian ferns to nimble vegetarian
        behemoth in the narrow lacuna begrudged us

by two Ford Explorer ads. Ten million years
    he thrived, he and his tribe—a passel of days
        munching shoots and fronds before the sky

charred, the waters rose, and when the pall
    at last lifted, men stood and soon were running
        their first crude spears through the chest wall

of their fellow bipeds, getting ever better
    at it over time, while back inside the cave
        women and children huddled and prayed

to whatever god or goddess should listen.

WESTERN HISTORY

—for Eleanor Wilner

In roughly 983 A.D., Gorm the Old (age 32)
united the Jutes and Angles beneath one flag
whose emblem of stag and sword and sun
stood for the anointing hand of the Divine.

The next king in our queue, Harald Bluetooth,
Christianized Denmark. Then we catapult
to medieval France, some distant descendant
of Pepin the Short or forebear of Robespierre

leading the fetid seeding of what will flower
into the City of Light. From the East swarm
Suleiman's sons, hell-bent for Vienna's gates—
it's 1648 by now, the *Pinta*'s planks long gone

to fire and drift, but spices, guns and slaves
will still be volleyed across the Atlantic
two more centuries, fleas and death hitching
their ride on the fine hairs of *rattus rattus*.

And just three hundred years, give or take,
until *bubonic plague* sounds almost quaint
before the ordered and more precise tunes
to be beaten out by spit-polished boots.

How much one wants to end it there,
among the charnel houses, ossuaries, ash
of the past, yet even a new millennium, lit
by halogen, linked by gigabyte, cannot hold

back the smart bombs and homemade grenades.

ANECDOTAL EVIDENCE

When I was eight and Fred was ten,
he taught me how to concentrate
sunlight in a magnifying glass.
We'd focus that golden shaft
onto the thorax of one of the many
busy ants crisscrossing the sidewalk.
Before the traffic light twice returned
to red, the ant had been congealed
to a black glob: no thorax,
no feelers, no legs, no eyes.
We ran our experiments until
Fred's parents called out time to go,
and one day they stopped
visiting my parents and I stopped
melting ants. I remember this
only now because I just read
Fred (now Frederic) is first cellist
with the Philadelphia Symphony,
and will be in town to present
a concert, his Austrian wife
accompanying him on piano.
Art ennobles life, I like to think,
then remember melting ants,
that Fred's mother survived Terezin,
and my shock last month, seeing
Hitler's watercolors, his deft
hand, his sure command of tone,
his vivid blues and greens.

IMMORTALITY

Gatling and Colt,
Mauser and Lüger,
Kalashnikov, Uzi—

you men of invention
live on in the hammer
and the grip, muzzle

and buttstock, bluing,
fire, recoil—wherever
you are, blood pools,

wound and clot
flashing the code,
your family name

shattering bone.

SIGHTING

I close my eyes again and see
the bulbous red clown nose
and wide sad smile of Emmett Kelly,
after the lion-tamer quits the cage
and the whip-cracks fade. What is it
about noses? There's a science
of noses, of calibrating origins
from shape and angle. In Istanbul
and Baghdad I've beheld beaks
magnificent as prows of ocean liners.
On a train years ago, three decades post-
War, two wizened Italian widows
asked my own nationality. American.
This was near Delft, carloads
of blue and white porcelain lighting
the souvenir shops. *No, no,* they rejoined,
their fingers metronomic ramrods
beneath my nose, *your nationality.*
(This in German, only language
we had in common.) Oh, my *nationality* . . .
Ich bin Jude (that *j* a *y* in the tongue
of Goethe). *Aha!—Isra-ëli.*
People tell me I look Italian. *Si,*
but not the nose. The fatal science held
elsewhere as well: across the broad face
of Mao's China the least indentation
beside the bridge branded those noses
that had once supported eyeglasses,

informing the Red Guards you could read;
and the aquiline nose of Sheba, so long
admired in the West, marked the Tutsi
in Rwanda for the machete and the grave.

KNOWING INSOMNIA

An ordinary man in a musty Bed
    & Breakfast imagines his wife, half
        a world away, in India, where the time

must be more or less 3 P.M., because for him
    3 A.M.'s second hand circles on relentlessly
        above a frameless scene: a distant sailboat,

tacking toward the horizon's blue filament.
    Were it a clock not a painting, that white boat
        would be headed toward 10, beyond the empty

stairway dropping away to the empty sea.
    This very moment she might well be seeing
        Delhi's Red Fort for the first time, the sun

searing the throngs, that man sprawled on his pallet,
    what remains of that man: wild mat of black hair,
        bare torso color of scorched copper, limb stumps

jerking in unison to the steady voice issuing
    from within, lungs to lips, lips to sun, chanting out
        in unmutilated certainty, *Allah, Allah, Allah, Allah.*

The husband hears it still, four years later,
    deep and resonant, *Allah, Allah,* everywhere
        torrents of shalwar kamiz, saris, English suits

parting about him, man on the pallet, lone island
    of ecstatic union, four quaking stumps upthrust
        toward twelve o'clock, toward the manifest truth

of the sun. As long as he lives the man who waits
    for sleep will see that scene, and he wonders if his wife,
        returned to her own time zone, will lie sleepless too.

CORRESPONDENCE

In the Hebrew of the Bible
and of today I understand

the di-syllabic word *adam*
is the word for man as well

so in the Arabic of the Koran
and of today must it not be

true that two like syllables
mean the same two things—

Adam, man—and don't *bin*
and *ben* both mean *son of*

PEACH TIME, NEPAL

Jammed between foes,
The Hindu Kingdom
seeks to be *A Zone
of Peach*. The King
proclaimed it himself.
Imagine all the peaches
bent low in a long line
of trees the long length
of the jagged Himalayas.
One foot ahead of the next
on the narrow trail, trekker,
porter, trader, *sadhu*, holy
cow—all stretching into
summer for a golden peach.
Base camp, Annapurna:
18,000 feet above distant
seas, China to the north,
India south, Pakistan
out there too, missiles
to the left of us, missiles
to the right, ice picks
and pokers, peach
in our time, nuclear
peach talks, take another
little peach of our heart.

DECIMATION

Not wholesale
  elimination, final
  solution—it's just
reduction by $1/10^{th}$,
not unlike the way
this eight-foot high
column of bleached
skulls from Pol Pot
days tapers upwards
almost imperceptibly
from base to topmost
crown, so as to mimic
the *stupa*, sacred tower
built over a lock of hair
or thread of robe or other
relic of the Buddha or spot
where once he'd meditated
during his life's slow journey
to enlightenment, his becoming
ever more serene, impermanent,
white rose above a lattice of bones

THREE

THE MYSTERY AND MELANCHOLY
OF THE STREET

Piano in Melanesian Pidgin is *big black box with teeth,*
you hit him, he cry. Must take forever to reach the end
of the sentence in Pago Pago. And why is Pago Pago
pronounced *Pango Pango*, like it rhymes with *tango*?
Where did that *n* go? If it's true the tango was invented
in Argentina a century ago, why's their economy
such a mess today and when will the Mothers
of the Plaza de Mayo get justice? All over the world
women are named for what blooms—*Daisy, Iris,*
Dahlia, Lily, Rose—but no man is named for a flower,
which explains a lot about human history. Lady Day
always wore a white gardenia in her hair, even though
she wasn't allowed up the elevator with white folk.
The *Infanta of Castille* may be the answer to the conundrum
of London's tube stop, *Elephant and Castle*, whose origin
otherwise—like ours—is an enigma, a vortex of mystery
that must perplex even the most jaded urban commuter.
I know it does me, these mornings when a humid breeze
bodes another scorcher in the City of Brotherly Love.
Wasn't Poor Richard lucky not to get himself electrocuted
flying his kites into those lightning storms, so later
he could have all his amorous escapades in Paris? A bad
bounce last night caromed me into the Emergency Room
with a busted clavicle. *No sweat, you'll be shooting hoops*
again in no time the intern opined, pulling her figure-
of-eight brace taut against my chest. But who can hear
the word *hoops* without immediately seeing that little blond girl
rolling her hoop up the ochre umber burnt sienna street
in Giorgio di Chirico's famous painting that portends
the rise of fascism in Italy according to art historians

because the scene is a rigid geometry of arc and angle
and her face is unseen, and though she seems carefree
in the Tuscan sun, she's rolling her big innocent hoop
into the looming shade.

JEWEL CASE

Too bad Freud's *Interpretation*
of Dreams—that complex logic
and infinitely mutable design
underlying his wielding the key,
his analysand the lock—never,
even in theory, could be disproved
(like every other religion,
but *verboten*, the death-kiss,
in science) and so in time
became passé, because of course
the 1920's upper-middle-class matron
who dreamed recurrently
in the depths of the Viennese
mittel-nacht that someone unknown
and sinister was stealing her *schmucken-*
casten in truth feared some man
wanted to steal her sexuality, her
personhood, her family, her core.
Perhaps those primitive tribes
who hold that dreams foretell
the distant and certain future
possess the correct cosmology.
After all, didn't elegant Frau M
lose more than her jewel-case
not too many years later
there where even the grass
was indelibly inked.

MOTHER TERESA AND I ARE
UPGRADED TO FIRST CLASS

An abrupt hush
descends and a host
of stares fix on me,
being led ahead. Irate
gray clouds press
the portholes. I fear
the smell of my fear
has been unloosed,
so quickly buckle in.
But it's the woman
behind me compelling
the eyes, the elderly one
in the whitened face
and certainty of a saint,
the frailty and the flint—
now I know I'm safe
on this leg of my flight,
even without kissing
her blue and white habit
like a prayer shawl.

ARDOR

No wonder *ardour* couldn't survive
the bullying linguistic fist of the Hero
of the Battle of San Juan Hill,
robust and lusty Theodore Roosevelt,
who also managed, upon becoming
the youngest and most virile President
of a young and expanding country,
to eliminate the *u* from the scents
of *arbour*, the necessities of *labour*
and *neighbour,* the cacophony of *clangour*,
the heat of *rancour*.
                         O Teddy, burly
bespectacled one, monumentally chiseled
into the granite of that mountainside above
the Badlands, see how the world has grown
harder to command than any Commander-
in-Chief could have imagined a century ago:
no Presidential declaration can alter the rules
of spelling, though it can still delete faces
that leave us with a last short *o* on their lips.

THE WORD

What will be the *modem* of the future,
that next newest word nonexistent

millennia past, routine as rain today,
in Amharic, Ibo, Quechua, Pashto—

in all the world's lacerated tongues—
our blue globe booted up, humming

like a giant hive, bits and bytes pulsing
Earth in less than a nano, unconnected

to spindrift, moonrise, pain. What word
will be used a century hence when someone

is asked have the empty belly and the bomb
yet gone the way of the sundial, the slave?

MOE

It's a truth undeniable:
it's The Three Stooges,
immortal in rerun,

who reveal the truth
of our world: not its lack
of decorum or sense,

nor that it surely belongs
to the strong and the brash;
not the Leader's numbing

fist pummeling his lackeys'
scalps; not the poking of eyes,
nor the crazed *nyuk-nyuk-nyuk*;

but that rare interlude
of tenderness, that pause
in the action when the lens

freezes the Leader's face—
suddenly, unaccountably
sad—and Larry and Curly

undergo epiphany: *Woe is Moe.*
Which, once uttered, changes
nothing, ending as it does

in masculine rhyme.

SOUND AND LIGHT

Aïda's across the street at the Odéon—
    not the Egyptian spectacle with elephants
        onstage, the Disney cartoon, dubbed in Greek.

The Parthenon's being strafed by light—
    not the wan light of the crescent moon,
        light of the nightly Sound and Light Show:

one hundred thousand watts beamed in turn
    to the pockmarked columns, portico, denuded
        frieze. The Golden Age of Pericles rises again

in surgical light, then falls once more
    into the arid Athenian night. Yesterday
        the loquacious Israeli masseuse practicing

Shiatsu on Santorini said a New Age
    is arrived, lion and lamb about to settle
        as one in Haifa, Hebron, Jericho, Jerusalem.

She'd met a Syrian, massaged a Jordanian—
    Love, she said, it's all we need. Everyone
        agreed, then dove into the turquoise sea.

Diving, thumbs up means big problem,
    must surface fast. Thumbs and fingers
        kissing in circles (she used that word:

kissing) means OK, let's keep flapping
    our fins like so many fish, keep those
        bubbles bubbling up, until our oxygen

runs down and we must leave the reef
    and rise to the light, light of the world,
        where millions of thumbs point up.

ONE ANOTHER

Another anapestic afternoon,
mutable tropical light softening
at dusk, silvery waves skittering in.

Poetry—read life—must
resist the intelligence almost
successfully, says Stevens, and today,

beneath the fronds that castanet gaily
in the humid breeze, it gives pleasure
too. What else is there for us, marooned

as we are on one shifting tectonic plate
or another, but this scintillating rush
of the good air lungward, the gold

glinting from the armadillo's shell?
People, stop shooting one another
I shout to the scavenging gulls,

the twining purple bougainvillea.

FOUR

GRACE

—Agha Shahid Ali, 1949–2001

I suppose it's only human
nature to use trade jargon
to signify one's membership

in the guild, possession
of the arcane and potent
lore of the few, the elect—

doesn't the alchemist wield
his *azoth*, the bishop his *ambo*,
his *ciborium*—thus the physician

masks the bitter draught
of diagnosis and prognosis
within an effusion of words

so sweet in their sonic grace
when intoned slowly enough,
slow as an agonal breath, long

words of ancient provenance
that bespeak the toga, the oracle,
the goddess, achingly beautiful

words, ewers into which are poured
long vowels and multiple syllables,
leukopenia, septicemia, glioblastoma.

WE CALLED HIM *DOST*

> *Those transparent Dacca gauzes*
> *known as woven air, running*
> *water, evening dew:*
>
> *a dead art now, dead over*
> *a hundred years . . .*
> —Agha Shahid Ali, "The Dacca Gauzes"

1. Dost

We called him *Dost,*
    Kashmiri for *Teacher*
        he'd said when asked.

(Later we learned it's *Friend.*)

He called us *Darling,*
    Shahidi for so much
        meant all at once—

not just the color
    but the word, *mauve,*
        with its hidden, lip-

tautening moan;
    how *vatic* rhymes
        with *dramatic, ecstatic*

and *asthmatic*;
    every line of Keats
        and Yeats (almost);

and the next laugh
    is coming, surely,
        any moment now.

2. He Loved with Glee

He loved with the glee of a child
the grand and the florid
way the flowing Himalayan robes
of his name caressed
our North American ears,
how its three initials formed
the same palindrome as did those
of the Acoustical Society of America,
and that *Asa* was not only a king
of Judah (*laid in his bed filled with sweet
odors and divers kinds of spices*) but also
the Zoroastrian principle of good.

3. Guru *in Urdu*

True, *Guru*
in Urdu's
not *Loulou,*
but *Boudu*
Saved from
Drowning's
at the Bijou—
this tourniquet
of *u*'s, continuum
ad nauseam,
can't stanch
the loss of you.

4. Sorry, This Is Not

Sorry, this is not, dost, a ghazal.
Though as you see, it's almost a ghazal.

What you taught us first, to rhyme
Ghazal with *nuzzle,* I shan't forget,

Nor the guttural aspirate that opens it.
Were this more than the ghost of a ghazal,

What would be its *radif* would end
Self-referentially, dost, at *ghazal,*

A Möbius-strip move that somewhere must be
Eliciting your Cheshire Cat smile (a boast, a puzzle)

At its self-referentiality, even though
This be but half—at best—a ghazal.

For one, the couplets fail to stand alone
The way you did, the last ghazal

Being leached from your brain. No, I will never
Master your Persian form—no simple host, a ghazal.

But the final couplet, the *makhta*, will contain the jewel
You left behind: your name, Shahid, your name.

THE DOG RACES IN FLORIDA

He can't stop thinking
        of his mother, contorted
                in her last bed, her voice

running to empty, able
        only to repeat *A point, I need
                a better point*, and unbidden,

he flashes to the dog track
        in Florida, the loudspeaker
                growling over its own static

Here comes Swifty—and they're off!:
        a mass of yelping greyhounds
                chasing that tiny tin rabbit

trailing the black Buick coupe.
        Around and around the tamped
                dirt the pack strains. Anyone

would have bet the dogs
        had learned by now no matter
                how fast they run, Swifty runs

faster. Then the point breaks
        clear: *They know, and run anyway.*

MOSAIC: ISTANBUL

1. In Transit

Beside me, on a black chair curved
like a scimitar, comes a pulse of *cheeps*
from an unaccompanied shopping bag.
Men from villages pace the *Room*
For Waiting: knit skullcaps, worn
worry beads, scarved wives wobbling
two steps behind. In crisp fatigues
the shade of late autumn, a bullet-eyed
soldier sifts the news for rumors of coup.
Döner kebap rotates slowly on a spit,
its juices pooling in a metal trough.
Hair cropped, dyed blonde, a city woman
returns to the bag, cracks a sunflower
seed and slides its shorn kernel
down into the bird's mesh cage.

2. Beyond

      the smoke-smeared window,
there where Asia starts, *Sahil Yolu*:
      the shore road. Oily
    tanker spume streaks the Marmara Sea.
         Minarets poise
upward into the heart
     of afternoon: rockets waiting
    for countdown. People everywhere—
families in outdoor tea houses,
    men fishing from quays,
      no one alone.

3. *These Little Flies*

that careless or in heat
I swat
from the hairs
of my forearms
are a tune
someone's mother hummed
in a kitchen long ago
to her son
as he clung to her leg
and she peeled potatoes
and the little flies
tasted first the salt
of his naked skin
and then the fried potatoes
and then the steak
before they all took
leave.

4. In the Courtyard of the Green House

Half an hour since my lover left—
thirty revolutions of the second hand—
and already her *Parting*

is the price of meeting has drowned
in the iron fountain, her laugh
lines and curled lashes as vanished

as the scene in sepia
on this souvenir postcard:
a middle-aged man, caught mid-

stride, mid-air, exits a wooden
streetcar into snow, whirling,
fat-flaked, scattered.

5. Roses

Every year
the roses return: amber,
garnet, ruby, jade.

They climb
the stone wall to the Palace
and peek in,

as if this is the time
foretold in the coffee grounds
when the *harem*

will walk again
beneath the arch of the sacred gate,
one of their number

plucked by the Sultan.

6. Lineage

Look into the face of this Hereke,
commands Kashif of Kashif's Carpets.
The slender stalks and pale leaves are trees
of life, the carmine border speaks of blood.

Fingers pulling wool through loom,
strand by coarse strand. Bowed child,
head scarved in modesty, a tendril
of hair escaping down her damp brow,
inward-turning eye squinting into
winter, just one last swath to weave
beneath Mother's anxious gaze
before the middlemen arrive . . .

The blue-black center holds the sea.

7. Dancing Bear

On the cobble path
between Ayasofya
and Topkapi Palace
a brown bear shuffles
behind a Gypsy youth.

The Levantine sun
glints off the bear's
brass nose ring,
startling the tourists
from their tales
of old Stamboul.

The bear does not
look left or right,
she just follows
the leather leash
wherever it leads.

8. Infidel in the Calligraphy Shop

This land: its eggplant, its noses,
    the caress of its lilting tongue
        in which my mother's name

means *mother*, and in every
    public place a picture of *The Father*
        of the Turks, as in this calligraphy

shop where the tourist can buy
    her name rendered in Kufic script,
        that classical Islamic hand he cut off

and dumped with the fez and dervish
    onto the Ottoman slag heap, its sinuous
        letters flowing right to left made to spell

Margaret or *Linda* or *Anne*. Or, should
    she prefer something more indigenous,
        she can have *Allah*, the ancient squiggle

hearkening us back well before Mohammed
    to Cleopatra and her asp, or *Insh'Allah—God*
        willing—in black ink massed as a closed tulip.

9. A Far Cry From Home

Five times a day, dark to dark, bursting
beyond its static, the muezzin's amplified call
arcs over tourist and Turk alike.

The rhythm of sands, of hawks and wells,
reverberates like blood in a three-chambered heart,
enters my arteries, murmurs

Even the now cannot be known.

I lay down my pen, remove my watch,
rise with the gulls to the minaret,
bend my wings to Mecca,

submit.

Notes

A Form of Optimism. This poem's title comes from a 1954 interview with Roberto Rossellini in *Cahiers du Cinéma*. His gritty and disturbing yet ultimately affirming *Open City*, filmed in 1945 shortly after the liberation of Rome, launched Italian Neo-Realism and was closely followed by other classics such as Luchino Visconti's *The Earth Trembles* and Vittorio De Sica's *The Bicycle Thief*. Of his work, Rossellini said, "I am not a pessimist; to perceive evil where it exists is, in my opinion, a form of optimism."

Emigrées. In the late 19th and early 20th centuries, the presence of signs of trachoma, a chronic contagious conjunctivitis, commonly resulted in refusal of entry to would-be immigrants to the United States. The disease, though preventable and now treatable, afflicts over 400 million people and remains the world's leading cause of blindness.

Knowing Insomnia. The *shalwar kamiz* is the traditional South Asian garment comprised of loose pants and long top.

Peach Time, Nepal. A *sadhu* is a wandering holy man, from the Sanskrit word for good, *sadhu*.

Mosaic: Istanbul. *Section 4*: Commander Mustafa Kemal, *Atatürk* ("Father of the Turks"), led the overthrow of the Ottoman Empire and founding of the Republic of Turkey. While the Republic's first President (1923–1938), Kemal "modernized" Turkey, secularizing government and education, Romanizing the alphabet, establishing equal rights for women, introducing Western attire, and banning the fez and the veil. *Section 9*: *Islam*, in Arabic, means *submission* or *surrender* (to the will of God).

A Note on the Author

Roy Jacobstein's first book of poetry, *Ripe*, won the Felix Pollak Prize and was a finalist for the Walt Whitman Award. His poetry appears in *The Gettysburg Review*, *The Iowa Review*, *The Missouri Review*, *Parnassus*, *Poetry Daily*, *Shenadoah*, *The Threepenny Review*, *TriQuarterly*, and elsewhere. He has received several awards from *Prairie Schooner* and *Mid-American Review*'s James Wright Prize. His poetry is included in the textbook *LITERATURE: Reading Fiction, Poetry & Drama* (McGraw-Hill, 2006). He has an M.D. and M.P.H. from the University of Michigan and an M.F.A. from Warren Wilson College. A public health physician and former official of the U.S. Agency for International Development, he works in Africa and Asia on women's reproductive health programs and lives with his wife and daughter in Chapel Hill, North Carolina.

A Note on the Prize

The Samuel French Morse Poetry Prize was established in 1983 by the Northeastern University Department of English in order to honor Professor Morse's distinguished career as teacher, scholar, and poet. The members of the prize committee are: Francis C. Blessington, Joseph deRoche, Victor Howes, David Kellogg, Ellen Noonan, Stuart Peterfreund, and Guy Rotella.